W9-CEA-960

THREE
MOMENTS
OF JOY

galison
www.galison.com f ◎ @galisongift
70 West 36th Street, 11th Floor
New York, NY 10018

Design by Katie Jennings Campbell
Embroidery by Walker Boyes
Images used under license from Shutterstock.com

ISBN: 978-0-7353-5504-0

First Edition: January 2018

Designed and printed in the United States of America.

10 9 8 7 6 5 4 3 2 1

THREE
MOMENTS
OF JOY

A Guided Journal for Recording
EACH DAY'S BLESSINGS

galison

What you focus on EXPANDS.

Every day of our lives is not a 24/7 party. We face challenges, heartbreaks, even devastation. But we also experience amazing moments of joy right in the midst of it all. That phone call or outreached hand that comes just when you need it. A sloppy, no-holds-barred kiss from a toddler or a dog. A sunset unlike any other you've ever seen before. The feel of your favorite blanket warm and comforting from the dryer. The sudden realization that a difficult time brought about a blessing in disguise.

Three Moments of Joy is designed to help you appreciate these moments that reflect the beauty in our imperfect lives, so you can get through all the other times that feel covered in mud (or even quicksand!). Spend some time jotting down your three best moments of joy every night before going to bed, and your eyes will be opened to all that your life has to offer. (You might even have trouble   narrowing your moments down to just three!)

Focus on the good—the gifts we are given each day—and you'll know the secret to living a full life.

THE MOMENTS
OF HAPPINESS
WE ENJOY
TAKE US
BY SURPRISE.
IT IS NOT
THAT WE
SEIZE THEM,
BUT THAT
THEY
SEIZE US.

— *Ashley Montagu*

Today's Date _____

My three moments of joy today:

1. _____

_____

2. _____

_____

3. _____

_____

Remember this,
THAT VERY
LITTLE
IS NEEDED
to make a happy life.

—Marcus Aurelius

My three moments of joy today:

1. _____

   _____

2. _____

   _____

3. _____

   _____

HAPPINESS,

not in another place,

BUT THIS PLACE...

not for another hour,

BUT FOR THIS HOUR.

—*Walt Whitman*

My three moments of joy today:

1. _____

_____

2. _____

_____

3. _____

_____

THE MOST
BEAUTIFUL
THINGS ARE
NOT ASSOCIATED
WITH MONEY;
THEY ARE
MEMORIES AND
MOMENTS.

—Alek Wek

Today's Date ....

My three moments of joy today:

1. _____

_____

2. _____

_____

3. _____

_____

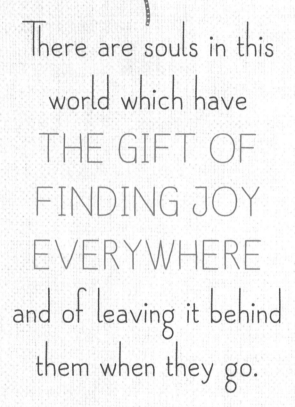

There are souls in this
world which have
THE GIFT OF
FINDING JOY
EVERYWHERE
and of leaving it behind
them when they go.

—Jean Paul

My three moments of joy today:

1. _____

_____

2. _____

_____

3. _____

_____

There is a calmness to a life lived in gratitude, A QUIET JOY.

—Ralph H. Blum

My three moments of joy today:

1. _____

   _____

2. _____

   _____

3. _____

   _____

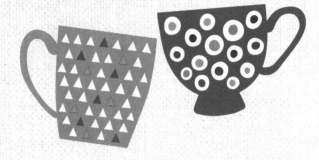

JOY COMES
IN SIPS,
NOT GULPS.

—Sharon Draper

My three moments of joy today:

1. _____

   _____

2. _____

   _____

3. _____

   _____

It is during our darkest

moments that we must

FOCUS TO SEE
THE LIGHT.

—Aristotle

My three moments of joy today:

1. _____

   _____

2. _____

   _____

3. _____

   _____

WE DO NOT
REMEMBER DAYS;
we remember
moments.

—Cesare Pavese

Today's Date _____

My three moments of joy today:

1. _____

_____

2. _____

_____

3. _____

_____

LOOK AT
EVERYTHING
AS THOUGH YOU
WERE SEEING
IT EITHER FOR
THE FIRST OR
LAST TIME.

—Betty Smith

My three moments of joy today:

1. _____

_____

2. _____

_____

3. _____

_____

I don't have to chase extraordinary moments to find happiness—IT'S RIGHT IN FRONT OF ME IF I'M PAYING ATTENTION.

—Brené Brown

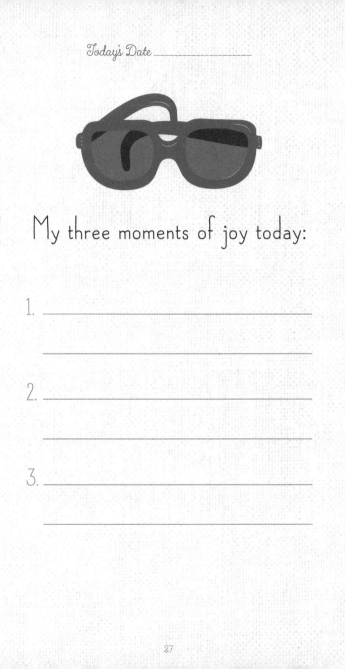

My three moments of joy today:

1. _____

   _____

2. _____

   _____

3. _____

   _____

SLOW DOWN
AND ENJOY LIFE.

It's not only the scenery you miss by going too fast—

YOU ALSO MISS THE SENSE OF WHERE YOU ARE GOING AND WHY.

—Eddie Cantor

My three moments of joy today:

1. _____

   _____

2. _____

   _____

3. _____

   _____

LIFE ISN'T A MATTER OF MILESTONES,
but of moments.

—Rose Kennedy

Today's Date ....

My three moments of joy today:

1. _____

   _____

2. _____

   _____

3. _____

   _____

We can choose to
FOCUS ON
THE BEAUTY
of the now.

—Steve Gleason

My three moments of joy today:

1. _____

_____

2. _____

_____

3. _____

_____

THERE ARE
MOMENTS
WHEN ALL
ANXIETY AND
STATED TOIL
ARE BECALMED
IN THE INFINITE
LEISURE AND
REPOSE OF NATURE.

—Henry David Thoreau

Today's Date _____

My three moments of joy today:

1. _____

_____

2. _____

_____

3. _____

_____

THE SUN DOES NOT
SHINE FOR A FEW
TREES AND FLOWERS,
but for the wide
world's joy.

—Henry Ward Beecher

My three moments of joy today:

1. _____

   _____

2. _____

   _____

3. _____

   _____

One doesn't recognize
THE REALLY
IMPORTANT
MOMENTS IN
ONE'S LIFE
until it's too late.

—Agatha Christie

My three moments of joy today:

1. _____

_____

2. _____

_____

3. _____

_____

Find joy

IN EVERYTHING
YOU CHOOSE TO DO.

—Chuck Palahniuk

Today's Date _____

My three moments of joy today:

1. _____

_____

2. _____

_____

3. _____

_____

SO OFTEN, WE
DON'T REALIZE
THAT THE VERY
MOMENTS IN WHICH
WE LIVE BECOME
OUR HISTORY,
OUR STORY.

—Deborah Wiles

My three moments of joy today:

1. _____

_____

2. _____

_____

3. _____

_____

A TABLE,
a chair,
A BOWL OF FRUIT
and a violin;
WHAT ELSE DOES
A MAN NEED
TO BE HAPPY?

—Albert Einstein

My three moments of joy today:

1. _____

   _____

2. _____

   _____

3. _____

   _____

You're only here

FOR A

MATTER OF

MOMENTS.

—Tim Conway

Today's Date _____

My three moments of joy today:

1. _____

   _____

2. _____

   _____

3. _____

   _____

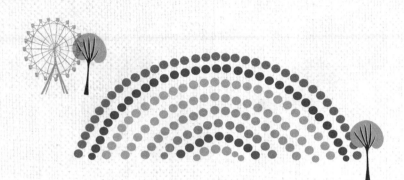

WE CANNOT
CURE THE WORLD
OF SORROWS,
but we can choose
to live in joy.

—Joseph Campbell

My three moments of joy today:

1. _____

   _____

2. _____

   _____

3. _____

   _____

WHAT IS
INTERESTING IN
LIFE IS ALL THE
CRACKS AND
ALL THE FLAWS
AND ALL THE
MOMENTS THAT
ARE NOT PERFECT.

—Clémence Poésy

My three moments of joy today:

1. _____

   _____

2. _____

   _____

3. _____

   _____

LIFE IS
A WAVE,
which in no two
consecutive moments
of its existence
is composed of
the same particles.

—John Tyndall

Today's Date ....

My three moments of joy today:

1. _____

_____

2. _____

_____

3. _____

_____

WE CAN ONLY BE
SAID TO BE ALIVE
in those moments
when our hearts
are conscious of
our treasures.

—Thornton Wilder

My three moments of joy today:

1. _____

   _____

2. _____

   _____

3. _____

   _____

YOU CAN SEE
AND YOU
CAN LISTEN,
BUT YOU HAVE
TO HAVE THOSE
MOMENTS
IN WHICH
YOU FEEL.

—Mike Krzyzewski

My three moments of joy today:

1. _____

_____

2. _____

_____

3. _____

_____

HOLD ON TO THOSE MOMENTS

when a little spark

cuts through the fog

AND NUDGES YOU.

—Rufus Wainwright

Today's Date _____

My three moments of joy today:

1. _____

_____

2. _____

_____

3. _____

_____

FIND THE
stolen
moments
OF JOY IN
ALL YOU DO.

—Niecy Nash

My three moments of joy today:

1. _____

_____

2. _____

_____

3. _____

_____

IF YOU
SURRENDER
COMPLETELY
TO THE
MOMENTS AS
THEY PASS,
YOU LIVE MORE
RICHLY THOSE
MOMENTS.

—Anne Morrow Lindbergh

My three moments of joy today:

1. _____

_____

2. _____

_____

3. _____

_____

Happiness is
not having
what you want.
IT IS
APPRECIATING
what you have.

—Anonymous

My three moments of joy today:

1. _____

   _____

2. _____

   _____

3. _____

   _____

Little moments
CAN HAVE
A FEELING
and a texture
THAT IS
VERY REAL.

—Ralph Fiennes

My three moments of joy today:

1. _____

   _____

2. _____

   _____

3. _____

   _____

THE
MOMENTS WHEN
YOU HAVE TRULY
LIVED ARE THE
MOMENTS WHEN
YOU HAVE DONE
THINGS IN THE
SPIRIT OF LOVE.

—Henry Drummond

My three moments of joy today:

1. _____

_____

2. _____

_____

3. _____

_____

PAY
ATTENTION

to the moments

when you've felt

on top of the world.

—Sebastian Stan

My three moments of joy today:

1. _____

   _____

2. _____

   _____

3. _____

   _____

PERFECT
HAPPINESS
is a beautiful sunset,
THE GIGGLE OF
A GRANDCHILD,
the first snowfall.

—Sharon Draper

✳

My three moments of joy today: ✳

1. _____

   _____

2. _____

   _____

3. _____

   _____

THERE ARE PLACES
AND MOMENTS IN
WHICH ONE IS SO
COMPLETELY ALONE
THAT ONE SEES
THE WORLD
ENTIRE.

—Jules Renard

My three moments of joy today:

1. _____

   _____

2. _____

   _____

3. _____

   _____

The most
pivotal moments
in people's lives
REVOLVE
AROUND
EMOTIONS.

—Brandon Stanton

My three moments of joy today:

1. _____

_____

2. _____

_____

3. _____

_____

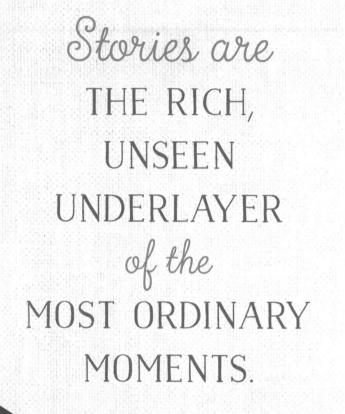

Stories are
THE RICH,
UNSEEN
UNDERLAYER
of the
MOST ORDINARY
MOMENTS.

—*Mary Gaitskill*

My three moments of joy today:

1. _____

   _____

2. _____

   _____

3. _____

   _____

JOY
IS NOT
IN THINGS;

IT IS IN
US.

—Richard Wagner

Today's Date ....

My three moments of joy today:

1. _____

_____

2. _____

_____

3. _____

_____

There are
moments when,
whatever the posture
of the body,
THE SOUL IS
ON ITS KNEES.

—Victor Hugo

My three moments of joy today:

1. _____

_____

2. _____

_____

3. _____

_____

THE REASON PEOPLE
FIND IT SO HARD TO
BE HAPPY IS THAT
THEY ALWAYS SEE
the past
BETTER THAN IT WAS,
the present
WORSE THAN IT IS,
and the future
LESS RESOLVED THAN
IT WILL BE.

—Marcel Pagnol

My three moments of joy today:

1. _____

_____

2. _____

_____

3. _____

_____

IT WAS
JUST ONE
OF THOSE
MOMENTS IN
THE UNIVERSE
THAT WAS
MINE.

—Carlton Fisk

My three moments of joy today:

1. _____
   _____

2. _____
   _____

3. _____
   _____

Those who wish
TO SING
will always find
A SONG.

—Swedish proverb

My three moments of joy today:

1. _____

_____

2. _____

_____

3. _____

_____

PLAY THE
MOMENTS,
pause the memories,
STOP THE PAIN,
*and rewind
the happiness.*

—Anonymous

My three moments of joy today:

1. _____

   _____

2. _____

   _____

3. _____

   _____

JOY IS THE
HOLY FIRE
THAT KEEPS
OUR PURPOSE
WARM
AND OUR
INTELLIGENCE
AGLOW.

—Helen Keller

My three moments of joy today:

1. _____

   _____

2. _____

   _____

3. _____

   _____

This moment

CONTAINS

ALL

MOMENTS.

—C. S. Lewis

My three moments of joy today:

1. _____

   _____

2. _____

   _____

3. _____

   _____

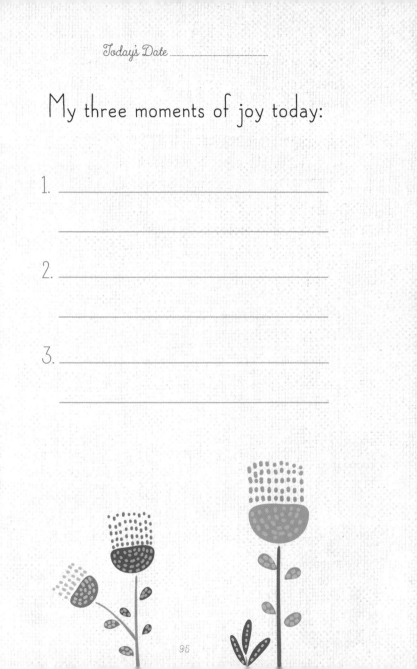

Folks are usually
about as
HAPPY
as they make
their minds
up to be.

— *attributed to*
Abraham Lincoln

My three moments of joy today:

1. _____

_____

2. _____

_____

3. _____

_____

NO MATTER
HOW HARD
TIMES GET,
THERE ARE
ALWAYS THOSE
MIRACLE
MOMENTS
THAT LIFT YOU
BACK ON YOUR
FEET.

—Anonymous

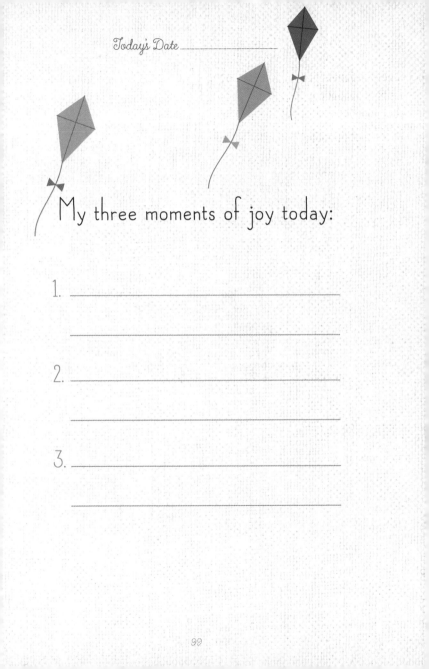

My three moments of joy today:

1. _____

_____

2. _____

_____

3. _____

_____

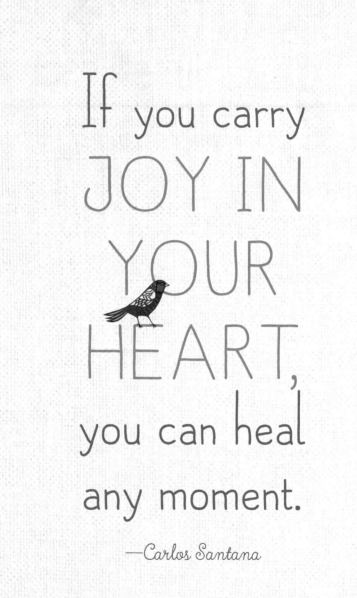

If you carry
JOY IN
YOUR
HEART,
you can heal
any moment.

—Carlos Santana

My three moments of joy today:

1. _____

_____

2. _____

_____

3. _____

_____

THINK JOY,
talk joy,
PRACTICE JOY,
share joy,
SATURATE
YOUR MIND
WITH JOY...

—*Norman Vincent Peale*

My three moments of joy today:

1. _____

_____

2. _____

_____

3. _____

_____

Who will tell whether one

happy moment of love,

or the joy of breathing

or walking on a bright morning

and smelling the fresh air,

is not worth all the suffering

and effort which life implies?

—Erich Fromm

My three moments of joy today:

1. _____

_____

2. _____

_____

3. _____

_____

COUNT YOUR LIFE WITH SMILES— NOT TEARS.

—Dixie Willson

Today's Date _____

My three moments of joy today:

1. _____

_____

2. _____

_____

3. _____

_____

The happiness
of your life
DEPENDS UPON
THE QUALITY OF
YOUR THOUGHTS.

—Marcus Aurelius

My three moments of joy today:

1. _____

   _____

2. _____

   _____

3. _____

   _____

LIFE IS
A JOURNEY,
and if you fall in
love with the journey,
YOU WILL BE IN
LOVE FOREVER.

—Peter Hagerty

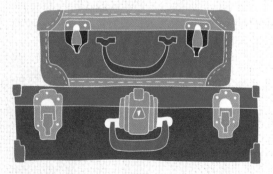

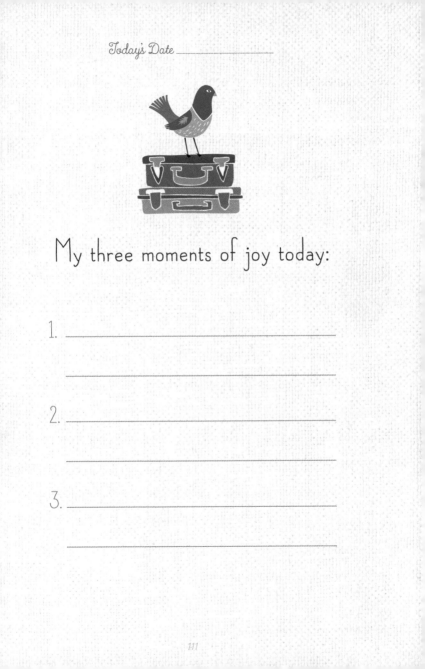

My three moments of joy today:

1. _____

   _____

2. _____

   _____

3. _____

   _____

IT ISN'T WHAT
YOU HAVE,
OR WHO YOU ARE,
OR WHERE
YOU ARE,
OR WHAT YOU
ARE DOING
THAT MAKES YOU
HAPPY OR UNHAPPY.
IT IS WHAT YOU
THINK ABOUT.

—Dale Carnegie

My three moments of joy today:

1. _____

    _____

2. _____

    _____

3. _____

    _____

IT'S A HELLUVA START,

being able to recognize what makes you happy.

—*Lucille Ball*

My three moments of joy today:

1. _____

_____

2. _____

_____

3. _____

_____

When one door
of happiness closes,
another opens,
BUT OFTEN WE LOOK
SO LONG AT THE
CLOSED DOOR THAT
WE DO NOT SEE THE
ONE THAT HAS BEEN
OPENED FOR US.

—Helen Keller

My three moments of joy today:

1. _____

   _____

2. _____

   _____

3. _____

   _____

EVERYONE'S LIFE HAS THESE MOMENTS, WHERE ONE THING LEADS TO ANOTHER.

—Peter Jackson

My three moments of joy today:

1. _____
_____

2. _____
_____

3. _____
_____

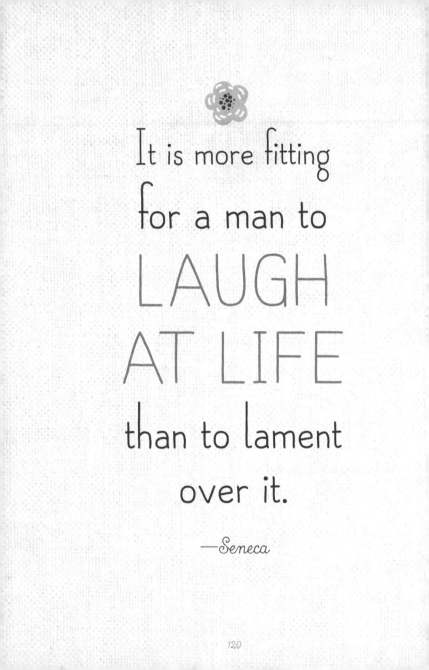

It is more fitting
for a man to
LAUGH
AT LIFE
than to lament
over it.

—Seneca

My three moments of joy today:

1. _____

_____

2. _____

_____

3. _____

_____

Life is really simple,

BUT WE INSIST

ON MAKING IT

COMPLICATED.

—Confucius

Today's Date _____

My three moments of joy today:

1. _____

_____

2. _____

_____

3. _____

_____

123

I REMEMBER
THE STORY OF
THE OLD MAN
WHO SAID ON HIS
DEATHBED THAT
HE HAD HAD
A LOT OF TROUBLE
IN HIS LIFE,
MOST OF WHICH HAD
NEVER HAPPENED.

—*Winston Churchill*

My three moments of joy today:

1. _____

   _____

2. _____

   _____

3. _____

   _____

The foolish man seeks
happiness in the distance.
THE WISE
GROWS IT
UNDER HIS FEET.
—James Oppenheim

Today's Date _____

My three moments of joy today:

1. _____

_____

2. _____

_____

3. _____

_____

HAPPINESS IS NOT THE ABSENCE OF PROBLEMS,

but the ability to deal with them.

— Charles de Montesquieu

My three moments of joy today:

1. _____

   _____

2. _____

   _____

3. _____

   _____

NO MAN IS HAPPY WHO DOES NOT THINK HIMSELF SO.

—*Publilius Syrus*

My three moments of joy today:

1. _____

_____

2. _____

_____

3. _____

_____

The greater part of
our happiness or misery

DEPENDS
UPON OUR
DISPOSITIONS,

and not upon

our circumstances.

—*Martha Washington*

My three moments of joy today:

1. _____

   _____

2. _____

   _____

3. _____

   _____

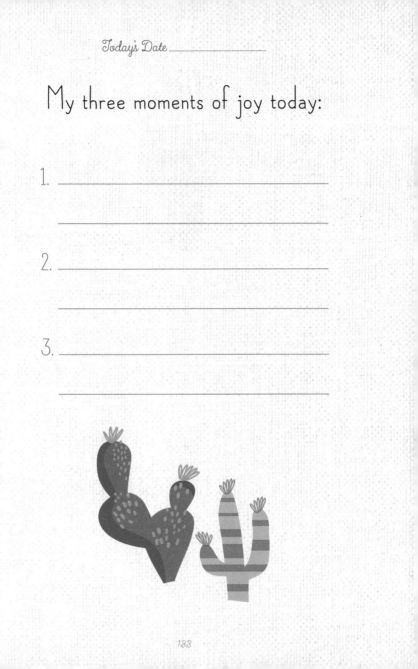

Just because it
didn't last forever
DOESN'T MEAN
IT WASN'T
WORTH YOUR
WHILE.

—Anonymous

My three moments of joy today:

1. _____

   _____

2. _____

   _____

3. _____

   _____

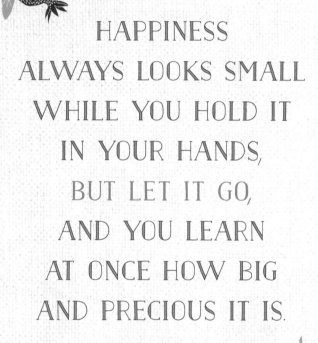

HAPPINESS
ALWAYS LOOKS SMALL
WHILE YOU HOLD IT
IN YOUR HANDS,
BUT LET IT GO,
AND YOU LEARN
AT ONCE HOW BIG
AND PRECIOUS IT IS.

—Maxim Gorky

My three moments of joy today:

1. _____

   _____

2. _____

   _____

3. _____

   _____

IN OUR DARKEST MOMENTS,

you have to find the humor, and you have to find the lightness.

—Corey Hawkins

Today's Date _____

My three moments of joy today:

1. _____

   _____

2. _____

   _____

3. _____

   _____

Plenty of people miss
their share of happiness,
NOT BECAUSE THEY
NEVER FOUND IT,
but because they
didn't stop to enjoy it.

—William Feather

My three moments of joy today:

1. _____

   _____

2. _____

   _____

3. _____

   _____

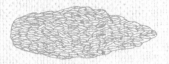

IF YOU ARE TOO BUSY TO LAUGH, YOU ARE TOO BUSY.

—Anonymous

My three moments of joy today:

1. _____

   _____

2. _____

   _____

3. _____

   _____

We don't always
choose moments...
SOMETIMES
THEY
CHOOSE US.

—Loretta Lynch

My three moments of joy today:

1. _____

   _____

2. _____

   _____

3. _____

   _____

IF...HAPPINESS
DEPENDS ON
a good breakfast,
FLOWERS IN
THE YARD,

a drink or
A NAP,
then we are more
likely to live with quite
a bit of happiness.

—Andy Rooney

My three moments of joy today:

1. _____

_____

2. _____

_____

3. _____

_____

SOME OF THE FUNNIEST, MOST BEAUTIFUL, AND TOUCHING MOMENTS

HAPPEN WHEN YOU LEAST EXPECT IT.

—Bryce Dallas Howard

My three moments of joy today:

1. _____

   _____

2. _____

   _____

3. _____

   _____

ENJOY
YOUR OWN LIFE
without comparing it
with that of another.

—Marquis de Condorcet

My three moments of joy today:

1. _____

_____

2. _____

_____

3. _____

_____

I AM
SENSIBLE
of the
VELOCITY
of the
MOMENTS...

—Harold Brodkey

Today's Date _____

My three moments of joy today:

1. _____

_____

2. _____

_____

3. _____

_____

OPTIMISM IS
A HAPPINESS
MAGNET.
IF YOU
STAY POSITIVE,
GOOD THINGS
AND GOOD
PEOPLE WILL
BE DRAWN
TO YOU.

—Mary Lou Retton

My three moments of joy today:

1. _____

_____

2. _____

_____

3. _____

_____

In the
quiet moments,
THE
DISCOVERIES
ARE MADE.

—Vera Farmiga

My three moments of joy today:

1. _____

_____

2. _____

_____

3. _____

_____

BEING HAPPY
DOESN'T MEAN
EVERYTHING
IS PERFECT.

*It means you've
decided to look beyond
the imperfections.*

—Anonymous

My three moments of joy today:

1. _____

_____

2. _____

_____

3. _____

_____

I AM
WORKING
ON FINDING
PEACE & JOY
IN THE
MOMENTS
WE HAVE
BEEN GIVEN.

—Taya Kyle

My three moments of joy today:

1. _____

   _____

2. _____

   _____

3. _____

   _____

If you spend your
whole life waiting
for the storm,
YOU'LL NEVER
ENJOY THE
SUNSHINE.

—Morris West

My three moments of joy today:

1. _____

_____

2. _____

_____

3. _____

_____

SHOW UP STRONG FOR THE MOMENTS THAT REALLY MATTER

with family, friends, and community.

—Andie MacDowell

My three moments of joy today:

1. _____

_____

2. _____

_____

3. _____

_____

LIFE WILL BRING YOU PAIN ALL BY ITSELF.

YOUR RESPONSIBILITY IS TO CREATE JOY.

—Milton Erickson

My three moments of joy today:

1. _____

   _____

2. _____

   _____

3. _____

   _____

Even in our
darkest moments
we try and find

SOMETHING

BEAUTIFUL.

—Eddie Vedder

Today's Date _____

My three moments of joy today:

1. _____
   _____

2. _____
   _____

3. _____
   _____

FIND A PLACE
INSIDE WHERE
THERE'S JOY,
and the joy will
burn out the pain.

—Joseph Campbell

My three moments of joy today:

1. _____

_____

2. _____

_____

3. _____

_____

THE BEST
MOMENTS
CAN'T BE
PRECONCEIVED.

—Brad Pitt

My three moments of joy today:

1. _____

   _____

2. _____

   _____

3. _____

   _____

Each day
HOLDS A
SURPRISE.

—Henri Nouwen

 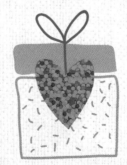 

My three moments of joy today:

1. _____

   _____

2. _____

   _____

3. _____

   _____

Moments like this
come and go
UNLESS WE
SEIZE THEM AT
THEIR HEIGHT.

—Jonathan Kozol

My three moments of joy today:

1. _____

_____

2. _____

_____

3. _____

_____

JOY IS A NET OF LOVE BY WHICH YOU CAN CATCH SOULS.

—Mother Teresa

My three moments of joy today:

1. _____

   _____

2. _____

   _____

3. _____

   _____

You get these
moments in the ring

THAT LAST

FOREVER.

—Sugar Ray Leonard

Today's Date ....

My three moments of joy today:

1. _____

_____

2. _____

_____

3. _____

_____

If the simple things
of nature have
a message that
you understand,

REJOICE,
FOR YOUR SOUL
IS ALIVE.

—Eleonora Duse

My three moments of joy today:

1. _____

_____

2. _____

_____

3. _____

_____

JOY IS WHAT
HAPPENS
WHEN WE
ALLOW
OURSELVES TO
RECOGNIZE
HOW GOOD
THINGS
REALLY ARE.

—Marianne Williamson

My three moments of joy today:

1. _____

   _____

2. _____

   _____

3. _____

   _____

Find what you
love to do,

FIND THE
JOY IN IT,

and express yourself
through your passion.

—Barry Williams

My three moments of joy today:

1. _____

   _____

2. _____

   _____

3. _____

   _____

We all find joy
and radiance
AND A REASON
TO MOVE ON
even in the
most dire of
circumstances.

—Ishmael Beah

Today's Date ....

My three moments of joy today:

1. _____

_____

2. _____

_____

3. _____

_____

STOP
AND TAKE IN
THE BEAUTY
OF AN
ORDINARY DAY.

—*Jennifer Garner*

My three moments of joy today:

1. _____

_____

2. _____

_____

3. _____

_____

Man cannot
live without
JOY.

—Thomas Aquinas

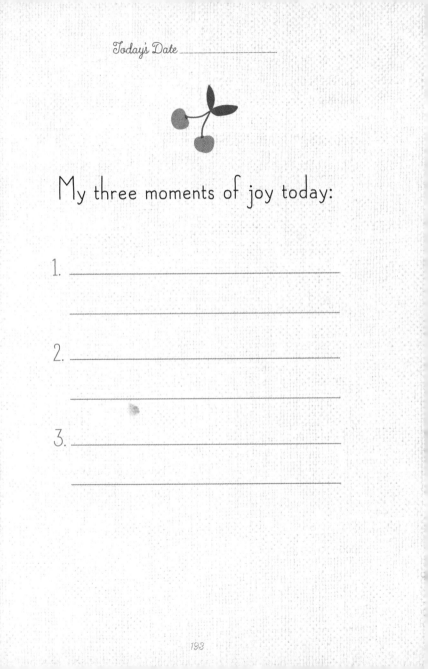

My three moments of joy today:

1. _____

_____

2. _____

_____

3. _____

_____

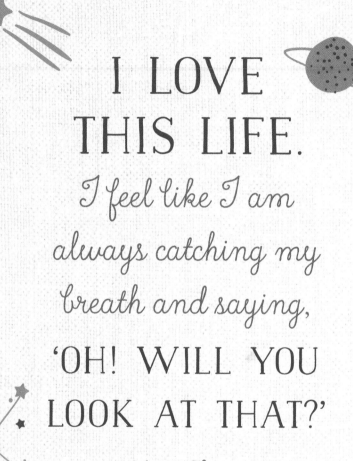

I LOVE
THIS LIFE.
I feel like I am
always catching my
breath and saying,
'OH! WILL YOU
LOOK AT THAT?'

—Harold Feinstein

My three moments of joy today:

1. _____

   _____

2. _____

   _____

3. _____

   _____

WE SHOULD
ALL DO WHAT,
IN THE LONG RUN,
GIVES US JOY,
EVEN IF IT IS
ONLY PICKING
GRAPES OR
SORTING THE
LAUNDRY.

—E. B. White

Today's Date ....

My three moments of joy today:

1. _____

_____

2. _____

_____

3. _____

_____

It is a fine
seasoning for joy to
THINK OF
THOSE
WE LOVE.

—Molière

My three moments of joy today:

1. _____

_____

2. _____

_____

3. _____

_____

JOY COMES
FROM PLACES
YOU LEAST
EXPECT IT.
*It's usually the
simple things.*

—Dave Gahan

My three moments of joy today:

1. _____

   _____

2. _____

   _____

3. _____

   _____

I'M TRYING
TO FIND A
LITTLE JOY
AND HAPPINESS,
A LOT OF
GIGGLES—
AND MAYBE
SOME PRETTY
SHOES.

—Tracee Ellis Ross

My three moments of joy today:

1. _____

_____

2. _____

_____

3. _____

_____

A DOSE
OF JOY
is a
spiritual cure.

—Ed Sullivan

My three moments of joy today:

1. _____

_____

2. _____

_____

3. _____

_____

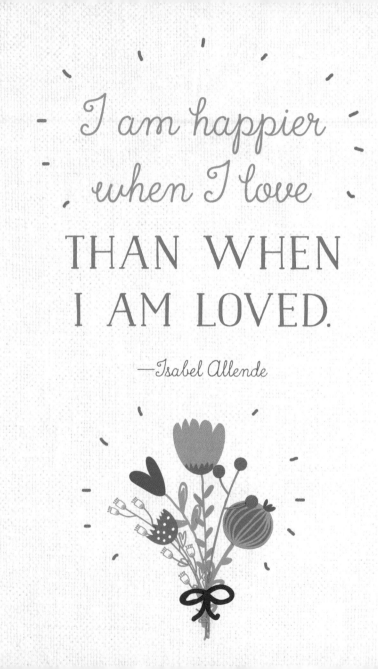

I am happier
when I love
THAN WHEN
I AM LOVED.

—Isabel Allende

My three moments of joy today:

1. _____

   _____

2. _____

   _____

3. _____

   _____

IT IS THE
EXPERIENCES,
THE MEMORIES,
THE GREAT
TRIUMPHANT JOY
OF LIVING TO THE
FULLEST EXTENT
IN WHICH
REAL MEANING
IS FOUND.

—Christopher McCandless

Today's Date _____

My three moments of joy today:

1. _____

_____

2. _____

_____

3. _____

_____

It's always such a joy
that you wake up
in the morning
AND THERE'S
WORK TO DO.

—Jerome Lawrence

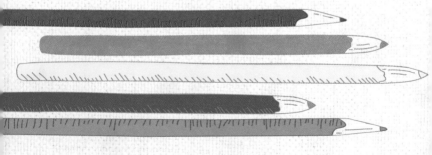

Today's Date _____

My three moments of joy today:

1. _____

   _____

2. _____

   _____

3. _____

   _____

If you emanate joy,
IT COMES
BACK TO YOU.

—Robin Wright

My three moments of joy today:

1. _____

   _____

2. _____

   _____

3. _____

   _____

GENUINE
HAPPINESS
COMES FROM
WITHIN,
AND OFTEN IT
COMES IN
SPONTANEOUS
FEELINGS
OF JOY.

—Andrew Weil

My three moments of joy today:

1. _____

_____

2. _____

_____

3. _____

_____

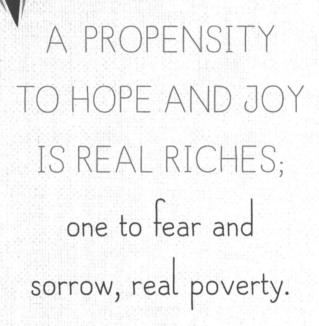

A PROPENSITY
TO HOPE AND JOY
IS REAL RICHES;

one to fear and

sorrow, real poverty.

—David Hume

My three moments of joy today:

1. _____

_____

2. _____

_____

3. _____

_____

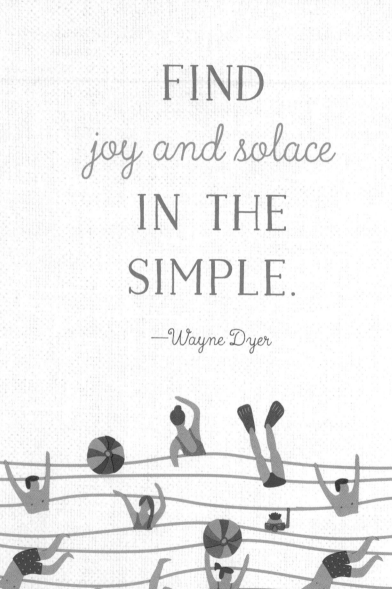

FIND
joy and solace
IN THE
SIMPLE.

—Wayne Dyer

Today's Date ....

My three moments of joy today:

1. _____

   _____

2. _____

   _____

3. _____

   _____

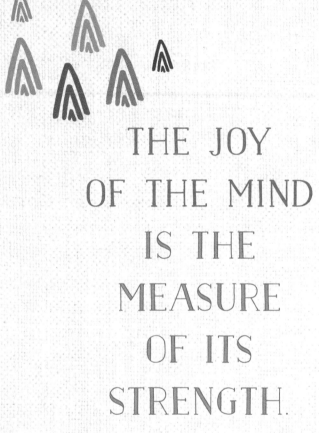

THE JOY
OF THE MIND
IS THE
MEASURE
OF ITS
STRENGTH.

—*Ninon de l'Enclos*

Today's Date _____

My three moments of joy today:

1. _____

   _____

2. _____

   _____

3. _____

   _____

JOY

is not the negation
of pain, but rather
acknowledging the
presence of pain
and feeling happiness
in spite of it.

—Lupita Nyong'o

Today's Date _____

My three moments of joy today:

1. _____

_____

2. _____

_____

3. _____

_____

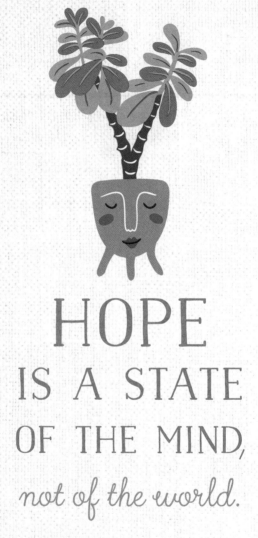

HOPE
IS A STATE
OF THE MIND,
not of the world.

—Václav Havel

My three moments of joy today:

1. _____

   _____

2. _____

   _____

3. _____

   _____

TO MAKE OTHERS
LESS HAPPY
IS A CRIME.
TO MAKE
OURSELVES
UNHAPPY IS
WHERE ALL
CRIME STARTS.
WE MUST TRY TO
CONTRIBUTE JOY
TO THE WORLD.

—Roger Ebert

Today's Date ....

My three moments of joy today:

1. _____

   _____

2. _____

   _____

3. _____

   _____

JOY IS THE WILL
WHICH LABOURS,
which overcomes
obstacles,
WHICH KNOWS
TRIUMPH.

—William Butler Yeats

My three moments of joy today:

1. _____

   _____

2. _____

   _____

3. _____

   _____

Side by side
with grief
LIES JOY.

—Fran Drescher

My three moments of joy today:

1. _____

   _____

2. _____

   _____

3. _____

   _____

THE SECRET TO LIFE

IS FINDING JOY IN ORDINARY THINGS.

—Ruth Reichl

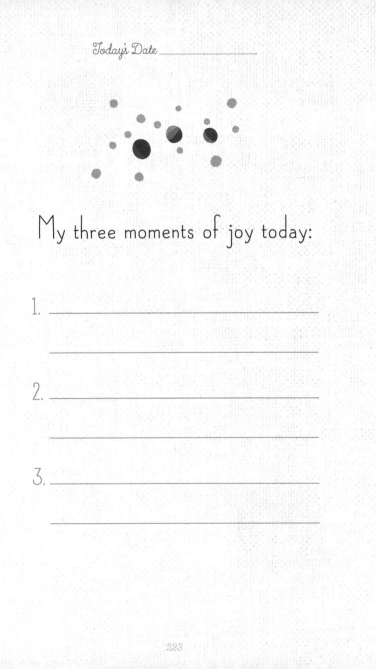

My three moments of joy today:

1. _____

_____

2. _____

_____

3. _____

_____

I choose to
spend my life
CRAFTING
A JOY.

—Jason Mraz

My three moments of joy today:

1. _____

_____

2. _____

_____

3. _____

_____

*Everywhere across
whatever sorrows
of which our
life is woven,*

SOME RADIANT
JOY WILL
GAILY
FLASH PAST.

—*Nikolai Gogol*

My three moments of joy today:

1. _____

_____

2. _____

_____

3. _____

_____

CONQUERING
ANY
DIFFICULTY
ALWAYS
GIVES
ONE A
SECRET
JOY.

—Henri-Frédéric Amiel

My three moments of joy today:

1. _____

_____

2. _____

_____

3. _____

_____

I believe
ENLIGHTENMENT
or
REVELATION
comes in daily life.

I look for joy,
the peace of action.

—Paulo Coelho

My three moments of joy today:

1. _____

   _____

2. _____

   _____

3. _____

   _____

MAKE SPACE
IN YOUR LIFE
FOR THE THINGS
THAT MATTER,
FOR
family and friends,

love and generosity,

fun and joy.

—Jonathan Sacks

My three moments of joy today:

1. _____

   _____

2. _____

   _____

3. _____

   _____

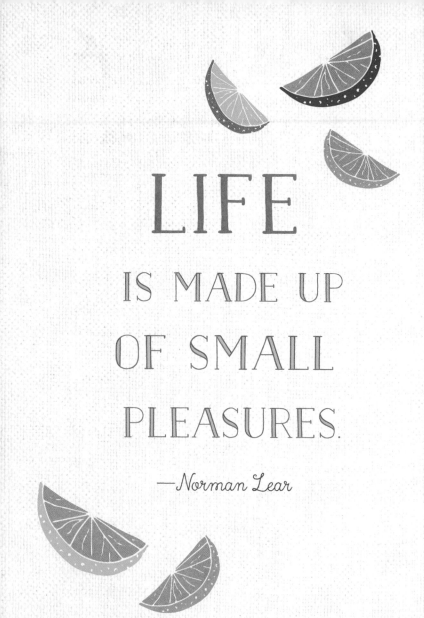

LIFE

IS MADE UP

OF SMALL

PLEASURES.

—Norman Lear

Today's Date _____

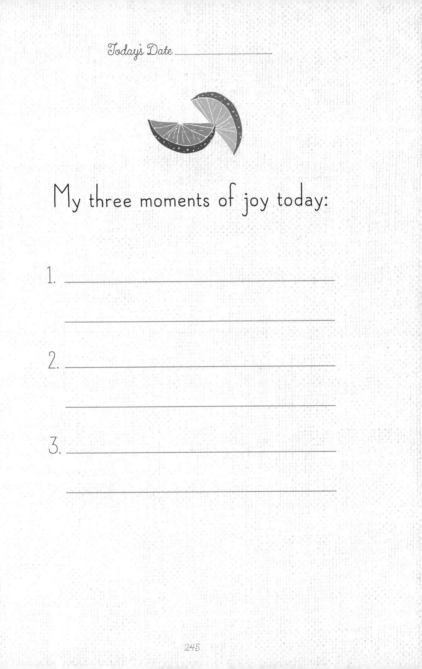

My three moments of joy today:

1. _____

_____

2. _____

_____

3. _____

_____

Do not be afraid
that joy will
make the pain worse;
IT IS NEEDED
like the air we breathe.

—Göran Persson

My three moments of joy today:

1. _____

   _____

2. _____

   _____

3. _____

   _____

I happy am,

JOY

is my name.

—William Blake

My three moments of joy today:

1. _____

_____

2. _____

_____

3. _____

_____

A LAUGH,
TO BE JOYOUS,
MUST FLOW
FROM A JOYOUS
HEART,
FOR WITHOUT
KINDNESS,
THERE CAN BE
NO TRUE JOY.

—Thomas Carlyle

My three moments of joy today:

1. _____

_____

2. _____

_____

3. _____

_____

It's a mistake
to miss out on
JOY
just because you
have pain.

—Taya Kyle

My three moments of joy today:

1. _____

_____

2. _____

_____

3. _____

_____

There is no
such thing as
THE PURSUIT
OF HAPPINESS,
but there is
THE DISCOVERY
OF JOY.

—Joyce Grenfell

My three moments of joy today:

1. _____

_____

2. _____

_____

3. _____

_____

JOY COMES, GRIEF GOES,

WE KNOW NOT HOW.

—James Russell Lowell

My three moments of joy today:

1. _____

   _____

2. _____

   _____

3. _____

   _____

I want to know
WHERE
JOY
LIVES.

—Goldie Hawn

My three moments of joy today:

1. _____

   _____

2. _____

   _____

3. _____

   _____

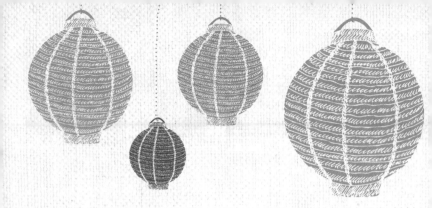

*One should
sympathise with*

THE COLOUR,

THE BEAUTY,

THE JOY OF LIFE.

—Oscar Wilde

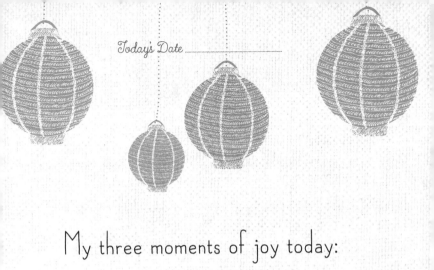

Today's Date _____

My three moments of joy today:

1. _____

_____

2. _____

_____

3. _____

_____

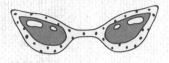

YOUR JOY COMES FROM HOW YOU THINK, THE CHOICES THAT WE MAKE IN LIFE.

—Joyce Meyer

My three moments of joy today:

1. _____

_____

2. _____

_____

3. _____

_____

When joy is a
HABIT,
love is a
REFLEX.

— Bob Goff

Today's Date ....

My three moments of joy today:

1. _____

   _____

2. _____

   _____

3. _____

   _____

We are all dreaming of some magical rose garden over the horizon— INSTEAD OF ENJOYING THE ROSES THAT ARE BLOOMING OUTSIDE OUR WINDOWS TODAY.

—Dale Carnegie

My three moments of joy today:

1. _____

_____

2. _____

_____

3. _____

_____

FOR IN THE
DEW OF
LITTLE THINGS
THE HEART
FINDS ITS
MORNING AND
IS REFRESHED.

—Khalil Gibran

Today's Date _____

My three moments of joy today:

1. _____

_____

2. _____

_____

3. _____

_____

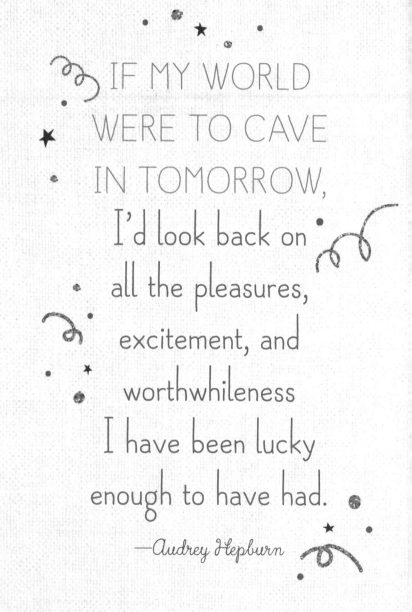

IF MY WORLD
WERE TO CAVE
IN TOMORROW,
I'd look back on
all the pleasures,
excitement, and
worthwhileness
I have been lucky
enough to have had.

—Audrey Hepburn

My three moments of joy today:

1. _____

_____

2. _____

_____

3. _____

_____

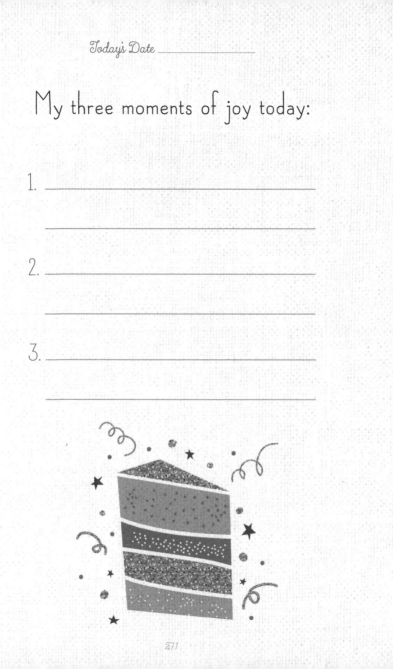

The present moment
is filled with

JOY AND
HAPPINESS.

If you are attentive,
you will see it.

—Thich Nhat Hanh